A Wainwright

A WALKER'S NOTEBOOK

F

FRANCES LINCOLN LIMITED
PUBLISHERS

Frances Lincoln Limited
74–77 White Lion Street
London N1 9PF
www.franceslincoln.com

British Library cataloguing-in-publication data
A catalogue record for this book is available
from the British Library

ISBN: 978-0-7112-3545-8

Printed in China
First Frances Lincoln edition 2007. This revised
edition 2014.

10 9 8 7 6 5 4

The fleeting hour of life of those who love the hills is quickly spent, but the hills are eternal. Always there will be the lonely ridge, the dancing beck, the silent forest; always there will be the exhilaration of the summits. These are for the seeking, and those who seek and find while there is yet time will be blessed both in mind and body.

I wish you all many happy days on the fells in the years ahead.

AWainwright

Looking backwards
(between one's legs),
there is a superb
upside-down view
of Wasdale Head

Finder, please return to

IN CASE OF EMERGENCY PLEASE CONTACT:

EMERGENCY CONTACT NUMBERS

For mountain rescue and coastguard help dial 999 or 112

OTHER USEFUL NUMBERS

WEATHER INFORMATION

It is easy to underestimate how quickly the weather can change, particularly if you are walking in hills, mountains and moorland. Before you set off always check the weather forecast and plan your route accordingly. If the weather deteriorates, turn back.

Always wear suitable clothing for your walk, including waterproofs. Waterproofs, gloves and a hat are easy to tuck into a bag 'just in case'. Likewise, if it is hot you will need to take sufficient water with you.

There are several national forecasting services but also many regional areas will offer local weather information.

The Met Office

www.metoffice.gov.uk
Provides a wide range of forecasts, and includes coverage for the National Parks and mountain areas.

[Note: The Publisher cannot accept responsibility for the content of any external websites.]

Mountain Weather Information Service

www.mwis.org.uk

Provides forecasts for eight different mountain areas in the UK as an aid to mountain safety. Forecasts can be downloaded as a pdf or accessed via a smart phone.

Mountain-Forecast

www.mountain-forecast.com

Provides detailed forecasts for more than 11,200 major summits around the world.

Snowdonia National Park

@safesnowdonia in English

@eryridiogel in Welsh

Social media is now being used to give visitors weather information and walking advice before setting off.

"Please can you tell me where the Pennine Way is?"

TRAFFIC & TRAVEL INFORMATION

The latest on road traffic and travel conditions is available from the following services. All calls are subject to a charge.

Road

Landline: 0900 3444 999 (RAC)
           0906 8884 322 (AA)
Mobile: Call 64644 (RAC)
           Call 84322 (AA)
           O2 Customers: Call Trafficline on 1200
           Vodafone customers: Call 2222
           T-Mobile customers: Call 2020
           Orange customers: Call 117

Rail

Network Rail for timetables www.networkrail.co.uk
National Rail Enquiries for reservations www.nationalrail.co.uk

Bus

National Express for coach travel www.nationalexpress.com
UK Bus Timetable website directory
www.showbus.co.uk/timetables

General travel

Travel Planning portal
www.traveline.org.uk

Admittedly, these illustrations have nothing to do with the Outlying Fells. Makes a nice change from drawing mountains, though.

USEFUL ORGANIZATIONS & WEBSITES

The following websites contain information on walking, destinations and equipment.

The Ramblers Association (Britain's biggest walking charity) www.ramblers.org.uk

The Woodland Trust (access details to over 1,000 woods) www.woodlandtrust.org.uk

The National Trust www.nationaltrust.org.uk

The National Trust for Scotland www.nts.org.uk

National Trails (information on 2,500 miles of trails in England, Wales & Scotland) www.nationaltrail.co.uk

The Ordnance Survey (buy or download maps online) www.ordnancesurvey.co.uk

Harvey Maps (for walking, hiking, rambling and cycling maps) www.harveymaps.co.uk

Walking Britain www.walkingbritain.co.uk

Walk Scotland www.walkscotland.com

Lake District National Park Authority www.lakedistrict.gov.uk

Cumbria Tourist Board site www.golakes.co.uk

Yorkshire Tourist Board site www.yorkshire.com

South West of England Tourist Board site www.visitsouthwest.co.uk

South East England Tourist Board site www.visitsoutheastengland.com

North East England Tourist Board site www.visitnortheastengland.com

Scottish Tourist Board site www.visitscotland.com

Welsh Tourist Board site www.visitwales.com

Ireland's Tourist Board site www.discoverireland.ie

NAISMITH'S RULE

Naismith's rule allows an easy calculation of the time taken for a hill walk, for a reasonably fit and steady walker. The rule was devised in 1892 by W. W. Naismith, a Scottish mountaineer.

The rule states that a fit person will travel at an average of 5 kilometres per hour, and will take an extra 30 minutes for every 300 metres of ascent.

For ascents you need to remember to take into account every metre climbed. For example if you ascend 100 metres, descend for 50 metres, and then ascend again for a further 150 metres, although you have only gained 200 metres of height, you have actually climbed 250 metres, and it is this full amount that must be taken into consideration.

Also consider that in poor visibility and rough terrain you will almost certainly move more slowly than the rule suggests, perhaps at 3 or 4km per hour. You will also travel more slowly at the end of the day.

Naismith's Rule should only be used as a rough guide and your estimate should take into account the prevailing conditions and should always be calculated for the slowest person in the walking group.

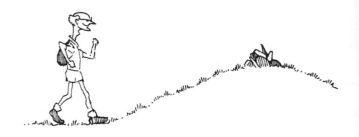

BEFORE YOU LEAVE – A CHECKLIST

- Water
- Food
- Plastic bag to carry your rubbish away
- Warm clothing
- First Aid kit including blister care
- Map
- Compass and navigation equipment
- Hat
- Gloves
- Sun protection cream
- Camera
- Torch
- Mobile phone (Mobile phone coverage in hilly areas can be very limited. You can check coverage before you go at: www.gsmworld.com)

Finally, have you left details with a third party of where you are going and when you are expecting to be back?

START LOCATION ....

DATE(S) WALKED ....

START TIME: .... FINISH TIME: ....

ROUTE/ASCENT(S)/DESCENT(S) USED

....

....

....

COMMENTS (walking companions, weather, observations, experiences etc)

....

....

....

....

....

....

....

....

....

....

....

....

START LOCATION ....

DATE(S) WALKED ....

START TIME: .... FINISH TIME: ....

ROUTE/ASCENT(S)/DESCENT(S) USED

....

....

....

COMMENTS (walking companions, weather, observations, experiences etc)

....

....

....

....

....

....

....

....

....

....

....

TAKE CARE
DO NOT
START
FIRE

and so waste the effort
spent in drawing all the
little trees on this map.
The Forestry Commission,
too, will be annoyed.

17

START LOCATION ....

DATE(S) WALKED ....

START TIME: .... FINISH TIME: ....

ROUTE/ASCENT(S)/DESCENT(S) USED

....

....

....

....

....

The

Caisteal
Abhail

Cioch
na h·Oighe

COMMENTS (walking companions, weather, observations, experiences etc)

....

....

....

....

....

....

....

....

....

....

....

n skyline, seen from Beinn Bharrain

START LOCATION ....

DATE(S) WALKED ....

START TIME: .... FINISH TIME: ....

ROUTE/ASCENT(S)/DESCENT(S) USED

....

....

....

COMMENTS (walking companions, weather, observations, experiences etc)

....

....

....

....

....

People with bad coughs should keep out of the line of fall

START LOCATION

DATE(S) WALKED

START TIME: FINISH TIME:

ROUTE/ASCENT(S)/DESCENT(S) USED

COMMENTS (walking companions, weather, observations, experiences etc)

The monument
(19th century)
marks the spot
where Henry VI
was found,
by shepherds,
wandering after the
Battle of Towton in
1461. He was taken
to the Castle and
sheltered there.

The monument

START LOCATION ....

DATE(S) WALKED ....

START TIME: .... FINISH TIME: ....

ROUTE/ASCENT(S)/DESCENT(S) USED

....

....

....

COMMENTS (walking companions, weather, observations, experiences etc)

....

....

....

....

....

....

....

....

....

....

....

....

START LOCATION ....

DATE(S) WALKED ....

START TIME: .... FINISH TIME: ....

ROUTE/ASCENT(S)/DESCENT(S) USED

....

....

....

COMMENTS (walking companions, weather, observations, experiences etc)

....

....

....

....

....

....

....

....

....

....

....

Circular sheepfold.
Wiley Gill

START LOCATION ....

DATE(S) WALKED ....

START TIME: ....   FINISH TIME: ....

ROUTE/ASCENT(S)/DESCENT(S) USED

....

....

....

COMMENTS (walking companions, weather, observations, experiences etc)

....

....

....

....

START LOCATION

DATE(S) WALKED

START TIME: FINISH TIME:

ROUTE/ASCENT(S)/DESCENT(S) USED

COMMENTS (walking companions, weather, observations, experiences etc)

START LOCATION ....

DATE(S) WALKED ....

START TIME: .... FINISH TIME: ....

ROUTE/ASCENT(S)/DESCENT(S) USED

....

....

....

COMMENTS (walking companions, weather, observations, experiences etc)

....

....

....

....

....

....

....

....

....

....

....

....

Malham Cove

START LOCATION ....

DATE(S) WALKED ....

START TIME: .... FINISH TIME: ....

ROUTE/ASCENT(S)/DESCENT(S) USED

....

....

....

COMMENTS (walking companions, weather, observations, experiences etc)

....

....

....

....

....

....

....

....

....

....

....

....

START LOCATION ....

DATE(S) WALKED ....

START TIME: .... FINISH TIME: ....

ROUTE/ASCENT(S)/DESCENT(S) USED

....

....

....

COMMENTS (walking companions, weather, observations, experiences etc)

....

....

....

....

....

....

....

....

....

....

....

....

Rock formations on Green Pikes

START LOCATION

DATE(S) WALKED

START TIME: FINISH TIME:

ROUTE/ASCENT(S)/DESCENT(S) USED

COMMENTS (walking companions, weather, observations, experiences etc)

Broad Stand

NOT FOR WALKERS

entrance

START LOCATION ....

DATE(S) WALKED ....

START TIME: .... FINISH TIME: ....

ROUTE/ASCENT(S)/DESCENT(S) USED

....

....

....

COMMENTS (walking companions, weather, observations, experiences etc)

....

....

....

....

....

....

....

....

....

....

....

HE'LL NEVER DO IT!

200

START LOCATION ....

DATE(S) WALKED ....

START TIME: .... FINISH TIME: ....

ROUTE/ASCENT(S)/DESCENT(S) USED

....

....

....

COMMENTS (walking companions, weather, observations, experiences etc)

....

....

....

....

....

....

....

....

....

....

....

....

START LOCATION ....

DATE(S) WALKED ....

START TIME: .... FINISH TIME: ....

ROUTE/ASCENT(S)/DESCENT(S) USED

....

....

....

COMMENTS (walking companions, weather, observations, experiences etc)

....

....

NO ROAD
TO THE LAKE

NO ROAD
TO THE LAKE

A negative signpost
(intended to help motorists)
Kirkstile Inn road junction

START LOCATION

DATE(S) WALKED

START TIME: FINISH TIME:

ROUTE/ASCENT(S)/DESCENT(S) USED

COMMENTS (walking companions, weather, observations, experiences etc)

START LOCATION ....

DATE(S) WALKED ....

START TIME: .... FINISH TIME: ....

ROUTE/ASCENT(S)/DESCENT(S) USED

....

....

....

COMMENTS (walking companions, weather, observations, experiences etc)

....

....

....

....

....

....

....

....

....

....

....

....

START LOCATION ....

DATE(S) WALKED ....

START TIME: .... FINISH TIME: ....

ROUTE/ASCENT(S)/DESCENT(S) USED

....

....

....

COMMENTS

....

....

....

....

....

....

....

....

....

....

....

....

Limestone pinnacle, Penyghent

START LOCATION

DATE(S) WALKED

START TIME: FINISH TIME:

ROUTE/ASCENT(S)/DESCENT(S) USED

COMMENTS (walking companions, weather, observations, experiences etc)

Ullswater
from the
north-east ridge

39

START LOCATION

DATE(S) WALKED

START TIME: .... FINISH TIME: ....

ROUTE/ASCENT(S)/DESCENT(S) USED

COMMENTS (walking companions, weather, observations, experiences etc)

Brae Fell
from the Caldbeck road
near Fell Side

START LOCATION ....

DATE(S) WALKED ....

START TIME: .... FINISH TIME: ....

ROUTE/ASCENT(S)/DESCENT(S) USED

....

....

....

COMMENTS (walking companions, weather, observations, experiences etc)

....

....

....

....

....

....

....

....

....

....

....

....

START LOCATION ....

DATE(S) WALKED ....

START TIME: .... FINISH TIME: ....

ROUTE/ASCENT(S)/DESCENT(S) USED

....

....

....

COMMENTS (walking companions, weather, observations, experiences etc)

....

....

....

....

....

....

Moss Eccles Tarn

START LOCATION ....

DATE(S) WALKED ....

START TIME: .... FINISH TIME: ....

ROUTE/ASCENT(S)/DESCENT(S) USED

....

....

....

COMMENTS (walking companions, weather, observations, experiences etc)

....

....

....

....

....

....

Wise Een Tarn

START LOCATION ....

DATE(S) WALKED ....

START TIME: .... FINISH TIME: ....

ROUTE/ASCENT(S)/DESCENT(S) USED

....

....

....

COMMENTS (walking companions, weather, observations, experiences etc)

....

....

....

....

....

The Pudding Stone
(the easy side)

It is perhaps
unnecessary
to add that the
figure up aloft
is not the author

START LOCATION ....

DATE(S) WALKED ....

START TIME: .... FINISH TIME: ....

ROUTE/ASCENT(S)/DESCENT(S) USED

....

....

....

COMMENTS (walking companions, weather, observations, experiences etc)

....

....

....

....

....

....

....

....

....

....

....

START LOCATION ....

DATE(S) WALKED ....

START TIME: .... FINISH TIME: ....

ROUTE/ASCENT(S)/DESCENT(S) USED

....

....

....

COMMENTS (walking companions, weather, observations, experiences etc)

....

....

....

....

....

Swindale
with *Selside Pike at the head of the valley*

START LOCATION

DATE(S) WALKED

START TIME: FINISH TIME:

ROUTE/ASCENT(S)/DESCENT(S) USED

COMMENTS (walking companions, weather, observations, experiences etc)

Swindale Head

START LOCATION ....

DATE(S) WALKED ....

START TIME: .... FINISH TIME: ....

ROUTE/ASCENT(S)/DESCENT(S) USED

....

....

....

COMMENTS (walking companions, weather, observations, experiences etc)

....

....

....

....

....

....

....

....

....

....

Path in the heather.
Caldew Valley
at the base of Knott
(Carrock Fell in the background)

START LOCATION ....

DATE(S) WALKED ....

START TIME: .... FINISH TIME: ....

ROUTE/ASCENT(S)/DESCENT(S) USED

....

....

....

COMMENTS (walking companions, weather, observations, experiences etc)

....

....

....

....

....

....

....

....

....

....

....

....

START LOCATION ....

DATE(S) WALKED ....

START TIME: .... FINISH TIME: ....

ROUTE/ASCENT(S)/DESCENT(S) USED

....

....

....

COMMENTS (walking companions, weather, observations, experiences etc)

....

....

....

....

....

....

....

....

....

....

....

....

from Gatherstone Head

START LOCATION ....

DATE(S) WALKED ....

START TIME: .... FINISH TIME: ....

ROUTE/ASCENT(S)/DESCENT(S) USED

....

....

....

COMMENTS (walking companions, weather, observations, experiences etc)

....

....

....

....

....

Gray Bull

Persons over 75 years of age
are advised to regard it
as unclimbable

START LOCATION ....

DATE(S) WALKED ....

START TIME: ....   FINISH TIME: ....

ROUTE/ASCENT(S)/DESCENT(S) USED

....

....

....

COMMENTS (walking companions, weather, observations, experiences etc)

....

....

....

....

....

....

....

....

....

....

....

....

START LOCATION ....

DATE(S) WALKED ....

START TIME: .... FINISH TIME: ....

ROUTE/ASCENT(S)/DESCENT(S) USED

....

....

....

COMMENTS (walking companions, weather, observations, experiences etc)

....

....

....

....

....

....

....

....

....

....

....

START LOCATION ....

DATE(S) WALKED ....

START TIME: .... FINISH TIME: ....

ROUTE/ASCENT(S)/DESCENT(S) USED

....

....

....

COMMENTS (walking companions, weather, observations, experiences etc)

....

....

....

....

....

....

....

....

....

....

....

....

START LOCATION ....

DATE(S) WALKED ....

START TIME: .... FINISH TIME: ....

ROUTE/ASCENT(S)/DESCENT(S) USED

....

....

....

COMMENTS (walking companions, weather, observations, experiences etc)

....

....

....

....

....

....

RED PIKE   SCOAT FELL   PILLAR   CRAG FELL

looking west

START LOCATION ....

DATE(S) WALKED ....

START TIME: .... FINISH TIME: ....

ROUTE/ASCENT(S)/DESCENT(S) USED

....

....

....

COMMENTS (walking companions, weather, observations, experiences etc)

....

....

....

....

....

....

looking south-south-east

START LOCATION

DATE(S) WALKED

START TIME: FINISH TIME:

ROUTE/ASCENT(S)/DESCENT(S) USED

COMMENTS (walking companions, weather, observations, experiences etc)

looking south-south-east
from Lanthwaite Hill

START LOCATION ....

DATE(S) WALKED ....

START TIME: .... FINISH TIME: ....

ROUTE/ASCENT(S)/DESCENT(S) USED

....

....

....

COMMENTS (walking companions, weather, observations, experiences etc)

....

....

....

....

....

....

....

....

....

....

....

....

START LOCATION ....

DATE(S) WALKED ....

START TIME: .... FINISH TIME: ....

ROUTE/ASCENT(S)/DESCENT(S) USED

....

....

....

COMMENTS (walking companions, weather, observations, experiences etc)

....

....

....

....

....

....

....

....

....

....

....

START LOCATION ....

DATE(S) WALKED ....

START TIME: .... FINISH TIME: ....

ROUTE/ASCENT(S)/DESCENT(S) USED

....

....

....

COMMENTS (walking companions, weather, observations, experiences etc)

....

....

....

....

....

....

....

....

....

....

....

START LOCATION ....

DATE(S) WALKED ....

START TIME: .... FINISH TIME: ....

ROUTE/ASCENT(S)/DESCENT(S) USED

....

....

....

COMMENTS (walking companions, weather, observations, experiences etc)

....

....

....

....

....

....

....

....

....

....

....

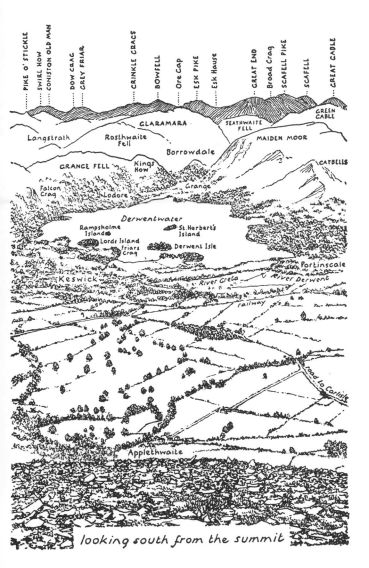

looking south from the summit

START LOCATION ....

DATE(S) WALKED ....

START TIME: .... FINISH TIME: ....

ROUTE/ASCENT(S)/DESCENT(S) USED

....

....

....

COMMENTS (walking companions, weather, observations, experiences etc)

....

....

....

....

....

....

....

START LOCATION

DATE(S) WALKED

START TIME: FINISH TIME:

ROUTE/ASCENT(S)/DESCENT(S) USED

COMMENTS (walking companions, weather, observations, experiences etc)

START LOCATION ....

DATE(S) WALKED ....

START TIME: .... FINISH TIME: ....

ROUTE/ASCENT(S)/DESCENT(S) USED

....

....

....

COMMENTS (walking companions, weather, observations, experiences etc)

....

....

....

*from Mungrisdale,
obviously*

(Telegraph poles removed from this view without permission of the P.O. Engineers)

START LOCATION

DATE(S) WALKED

START TIME: FINISH TIME:

ROUTE/ASCENT(S)/DESCENT(S) USED

COMMENTS (walking companions, weather, observations, experiences etc)

START LOCATION ....

DATE(S) WALKED ....

START TIME: .... FINISH TIME: ....

ROUTE/ASCENT(S)/DESCENT(S) USED

....

....

....

COMMENTS (walking companions, weather, observations, experiences etc)

....

....

....

....

....

....

On the top of
Binsey..........

..... Prehistoric
Tumulus
and
Ancient
Briton

START LOCATION ....

DATE(S) WALKED ....

START TIME: .... FINISH TIME: ....

ROUTE/ASCENT(S)/DESCENT(S) USED

....

....

....

COMMENTS (walking companions, weather, observations, experiences etc)

....

....

....

....

....

....

....

....

....

....

....

START LOCATION ....

DATE(S) WALKED ....

START TIME: .... FINISH TIME: ....

ROUTE/ASCENT(S)/DESCENT(S) USED

....

....

....

COMMENTS (walking companions, weather, observations, experiences etc)

....

....

....

....

....

....

....

....

....

....

....

START LOCATION

DATE(S) WALKED

START TIME: FINISH TIME:

ROUTE/ASCENT(S)/DESCENT(S) USED

COMMENTS (walking companions, weather, observations, experiences etc)

High Sweden Bridge

START LOCATION ....

DATE(S) WALKED ....

START TIME: .... FINISH TIME: ....

ROUTE/ASCENT(S)/DESCENT(S) USED

....

....

....

COMMENTS (walking companions, weather, observations, experiences etc)

....

....

....

....

....

....

Grasmere
from Loughrigg Terrace

START LOCATION ....

DATE(S) WALKED ....

START TIME: .... FINISH TIME: ....

ROUTE/ASCENT(S)/DESCENT(S) USED

....

....

....

COMMENTS (walking companions, weather, observations, experiences etc)

....

....

....

....

....

....

....

....

....

....

....

....

START LOCATION ....

DATE(S) WALKED ....

START TIME: .... FINISH TIME: ....

ROUTE/ASCENT(S)/DESCENT(S) USED

....

....

....

COMMENTS (walking companions, weather, observations, experiences etc)

....

....

....

....

....

....

....

....

....

....

....

Haweswater
from the third cairn

START LOCATION ....

DATE(S) WALKED ....

START TIME: .... FINISH TIME: ....

ROUTE/ASCENT(S)/DESCENT(S) USED

....

....

....

COMMENTS (walking companions, weather, observations, experiences etc)

....

....

....

....

....

....

....

....

....

....

....

....

START LOCATION ....

DATE(S) WALKED ....

START TIME: .... FINISH TIME: ....

ROUTE/ASCENT(S)/DESCENT(S) USED

....

....

....

COMMENTS (walking companions, weather, observations, experiences etc)

....

....

....

....

....

THE SUMMIT

Tourists looking for Blackpool Tower ↓

Boy Scouts

Typical summit scene

Solitary fellwalker, bless him, looking north to the hills

START LOCATION ....

DATE(S) WALKED ....

START TIME: .... FINISH TIME: ....

ROUTE/ASCENT(S)/DESCENT(S) USED

....

....

....

COMMENTS (walking companions, weather, observations, experiences etc)

....

....

....

....

....

....

....

....

....

....

....

START LOCATION ....

DATE(S) WALKED ....

START TIME: .... FINISH TIME: ....

ROUTE/ASCENT(S)/DESCENT(S) USED

....

....

....

COMMENTS (walking companions, weather, observations, experiences etc)

....

....

....

....

....

....

....

....

....

....

....

Cloven Stone

START LOCATION ....

DATE(S) WALKED ....

START TIME: .... FINISH TIME: ....

ROUTE/ASCENT(S)/DESCENT(S) USED

....

....

....

COMMENTS (walking companions, weather, observations, experiences etc)

....

....

....

....

....

The summit, from Striding Edge

START LOCATION ....

DATE(S) WALKED ....

START TIME: .... FINISH TIME: ....

ROUTE/ASCENT(S)/DESCENT(S) USED

....

....

....

COMMENTS (walking companions, weather, observations, experiences etc)

....

....

....

....

....

....

....

....

....

....

....

....

START LOCATION ....

DATE(S) WALKED ....

START TIME: .... FINISH TIME: ....

ROUTE/ASCENT(S)/DESCENT(S) USED

....

....

....

COMMENTS (walking companions, weather, observations, experiences etc)

....

....

....

....

....

....

....

....

....

....

....

START LOCATION ....

DATE(S) WALKED ....

START TIME: .... FINISH TIME: ....

ROUTE/ASCENT(S)/DESCENT(S) USED

....

....

....

COMMENTS (walking companions, weather, observations, experiences etc)

....

....

Napes
Needle

definitely
← not the
author!

START LOCATION ....

DATE(S) WALKED ....

START TIME: .... FINISH TIME: ....

ROUTE/ASCENT(S)/DESCENT(S) USED

....

....

....

COMMENTS (walking companions, weather, observations, experiences etc)

....

....

....

....

....

....

....

....

....

....

START LOCATION ....

DATE(S) WALKED ....

START TIME: .... FINISH TIME: ....

ROUTE/ASCENT(S)/DESCENT(S) USED

....

....

....

COMMENTS (walking companions, weather, observations, experiences etc)

....

....

....

....

....

....

....

....

....

....

....

....

Red Deer Stag

START LOCATION

DATE(S) WALKED

START TIME: FINISH TIME:

ROUTE/ASCENT(S)/DESCENT(S) USED

COMMENTS (walking companions, weather, observations, experiences etc)

400

START LOCATION ....

DATE(S) WALKED ....

START TIME: .... FINISH TIME: ....

ROUTE/ASCENT(S)/DESCENT(S) USED

....

....

....

COMMENTS (walking companions, weather, observations, experiences etc)

....

....

....

....

....

....

....

"... a massive heap of stones
calls for investigation ...."

What is its purpose, if any?
It is not a tumulus.
It is not a cairn.
It is not a wall.
It is not a bield.
It is not indicated on Ordnance maps.
It has an air of permanence but not of antiquity.
It could be nothing more than a collection of stones
  cleared from the adjacent forest in the course of planting.

START LOCATION ....

DATE(S) WALKED ....

START TIME: .... FINISH TIME: ....

ROUTE/ASCENT(S)/DESCENT(S) USED

....

....

....

COMMENTS (walking companions, weather, observations, experiences etc)

....

....

....

....

....

....

....

....

....

....

....

....

START LOCATION ....

DATE(S) WALKED ....

START TIME: .... FINISH TIME: ....

ROUTE/ASCENT(S)/DESCENT(S) USED

....

....

....

COMMENTS (walking companions, weather, observations, experiences etc)

....

....

....

....

The Wall on Cuddy's Crags
looking east to Housesteads Crags

START LOCATION ....

DATE(S) WALKED ....

START TIME: .... FINISH TIME: ....

ROUTE/ASCENT(S)/DESCENT(S) USED

....

....

....

COMMENTS (walking companions, weather, observations, experiences etc)

....

....

....

....

....

....

....

....

....

....

....

START LOCATION ....

DATE(S) WALKED ....

START TIME: .... FINISH TIME: ....

ROUTE/ASCENT(S)/DESCENT(S) USED

....

....

....

COMMENTS (walking companions, weather, observations, experiences etc)

....

....

....

....

....

....

....

....

....

....

....

START LOCATION ....

DATE(S) WALKED ....

START TIME: .... FINISH TIME: ....

ROUTE/ASCENT(S)/DESCENT(S) USED

....
....
....

COMMENTS (walking companions, weather, observations, experiences etc)

....
....
....
....
....
....
....

Derelict cottage and air shaft,
Lambley Colliery

START LOCATION ....

DATE(S) WALKED ....

START TIME: .... FINISH TIME: ....

ROUTE/ASCENT(S)/DESCENT(S) USED

....

....

....

COMMENTS (walking companions, weather, observations, experiences etc)

....

....

....

....

....

....

....

....

....

....

....

START LOCATION ....

DATE(S) WALKED ....

START TIME: .... FINISH TIME: ....

ROUTE/ASCENT(S)/DESCENT(S) USED

....

....

....

COMMENTS (walking companions, weather, observations, experiences etc)

....

....

....

....

....

....

The profile of High Spy looking south

HIGH SPY

Low Scawdel

CASTLE CRAG

Borrowdale

If a visitor to Lakeland has only two or three hours to spare, poor fellow, yet desperately wants to reach a summit and take back an enduring memory of the beauty and atmosphere of the district............... let him climb Castle Crag.

START LOCATION ....

DATE(S) WALKED ....

START TIME: .... FINISH TIME: ....

ROUTE/ASCENT(S)/DESCENT(S) USED

....

....

....

COMMENTS (walking companions, weather, observations, experiences etc)

....

....

....

....

....

Skye : The Old Man of Storr
and his family

START LOCATION ....

DATE(S) WALKED ....

START TIME: .... FINISH TIME: ....

ROUTE/ASCENT(S)/DESCENT(S) USED

....

....

....

COMMENTS (walking companions, weather, observations, experiences etc)

....

....

....

....

....

....

....

....

....

....

....

START LOCATION ....

DATE(S) WALKED ....

START TIME: .... FINISH TIME: ....

ROUTE/ASCENT(S)/DESCENT(S) USED

....

....

....

COMMENTS (walking companions, weather, observations, experiences etc)

....

....

....

....

....

....

....

....

....

....

....

....

Dovedale

START LOCATION

DATE(S) WALKED

START TIME: FINISH TIME:

ROUTE/ASCENT(S)/DESCENT(S) USED

COMMENTS (walking companions, weather, observations, experiences etc)

Crag End Beacon

START LOCATION ....

DATE(S) WALKED ....

START TIME: .... FINISH TIME: ....

ROUTE/ASCENT(S)/DESCENT(S) USED

....

....

....

COMMENTS (walking companions, weather, observations, experiences etc)

....

....

....

....

....

....

....

....

....

....

....

START LOCATION ....

DATE(S) WALKED ....

START TIME: .... FINISH TIME: ....

ROUTE/ASCENT(S)/DESCENT(S) USED

....

....

....

COMMENTS (walking companions, weather, observations, experiences etc)

....

....

....

....

....

....

....

....

....

....

....

START LOCATION

DATE(S) WALKED

START TIME: FINISH TIME:

ROUTE/ASCENT(S)/DESCENT(S) USED

COMMENTS (walking companions, weather, observations, experiences etc)

This full-length view of Thirlmere is excellent. By a cautious scramble a dramatic aerial prospect of the dam directly below may be obtained, but extreme care is necessary here: the precipice falls away suddenly and vertically.

START LOCATION ....

DATE(S) WALKED ....

START TIME: .... FINISH TIME: ....

ROUTE/ASCENT(S)/DESCENT(S) USED

....

....

....

COMMENTS (walking companions, weather, observations, experiences etc)

....

....

....

....

....

....

Entrance to Wark Forest

START LOCATION ....

DATE(S) WALKED ....

START TIME: .... FINISH TIME: ....

ROUTE/ASCENT(S)/DESCENT(S) USED

....

....

....

COMMENTS (walking companions, weather, observations, experiences etc)

....

....

....

....

....

....

....

....

....

....

....

....

START LOCATION ....

DATE(S) WALKED ....

START TIME: .... FINISH TIME: ....

ROUTE/ASCENT(S)/DESCENT(S) USED

....

....

....

COMMENTS (walking companions, weather, observations, experiences etc)

....

....

....

....

....

....

....

....

....

....

....

Bassenthwaite, from Ullock Pike

START LOCATION

DATE(S) WALKED

START TIME: FINISH TIME:

ROUTE/ASCENT(S)/DESCENT(S) USED

COMMENTS (walking companions, weather, observations, experiences etc)

ASCENT FROM BINSEY LODGE
620 feet of ascent : 1 mile

BINSEY

1400

heather

heather

1300

1200

Start the climb from a sheep-pen (two gates) off the Bewaldeth road. A sketchy track will soon be picked up, but when it ceases to gain height leave it and make for the top.

1100

bracken

Occasional boulders met on the ascent make comfortable seats for the weary

1000

Binsey Lodge

IREBY 2

900

Binsey Cottage

BEWALDETH 1¾

ULDALE 1½

800

Good fellwalkers, like good mountaineers, never walk where they can ride. Bus No. 71 goes past the Lodge.

OVER WATER 1

CASTLE INN 2

looking west·north·west

This gentle uphill walk is quite as easy, but somewhat longer, than appearances suggest. The summit is not in view from Binsey Lodge.

START LOCATION ....

DATE(S) WALKED ....

START TIME: .... FINISH TIME: ....

ROUTE/ASCENT(S)/DESCENT(S) USED

....

....

....

COMMENTS (walking companions, weather, observations, experiences etc)

....

Honister Crag

START LOCATION ....

DATE(S) WALKED ....

START TIME: .... FINISH TIME: ....

ROUTE/ASCENT(S)/DESCENT(S) USED

....

....

....

COMMENTS (walking companions, weather, observations, experiences etc)

....

....

....

....

....

....

....

....

....

....

....

START LOCATION ....

DATE(S) WALKED ....

START TIME: .... FINISH TIME: ....

ROUTE/ASCENT(S)/DESCENT(S) USED

....

....

....

COMMENTS (walking companions, weather, observations, experiences etc)

....

....

....

....

from Lanefoot

cows
sitting down
(explanatory note)

START LOCATION ....

DATE(S) WALKED ....

START TIME: .... FINISH TIME: ....

ROUTE/ASCENT(S)/DESCENT(S) USED

....

....

....

COMMENTS (walking companions, weather, observations, experiences etc)

....

....

....

....

....

....

....

....

....

....

....

START LOCATION ....

DATE(S) WALKED ....

START TIME: .... FINISH TIME: ....

ROUTE/ASCENT(S)/DESCENT(S) USED

....

....

....

COMMENTS (walking companions, weather, observations, experiences etc)

....

....

....

....

....

....

....

....

....

....

....

....

Patterdale

START LOCATION ....

DATE(S) WALKED ....

START TIME: .... FINISH TIME: ....

ROUTE/ASCENT(S)/DESCENT(S) USED

....

....

....

COMMENTS (walking companions, weather, observations, experiences etc)

....

....

....

....

....

....

....

....

....

....

....

....

START LOCATION ....

DATE(S) WALKED ....

START TIME: .... FINISH TIME: ....

ROUTE/ASCENT(S)/DESCENT(S) USED

....

....

....

COMMENTS (walking companions, weather, observations, experiences etc)

....

....

....

" .... a lovely peep around a corner...."
(direct ascent from Loweswater)

START LOCATION

DATE(S) WALKED

START TIME: FINISH TIME:

ROUTE/ASCENT(S)/DESCENT(S) USED

COMMENTS (walking companions, weather, observations, experiences etc)

the Kinniside Stone Circle

looking north.east

Knock Murton   BLAKE FELL   CAVEL FELL   HOPEGILL   GRASMOOR
                                                HEAD

START LOCATION ....

DATE(S) WALKED ....

START TIME: .... FINISH TIME: ....

ROUTE/ASCENT(S)/DESCENT(S) USED

....

....

....

COMMENTS (walking companions, weather, observations, experiences etc)

....

....

....

....

....

....

....

It is a remarkable fact that the Kinniside Stone Circle, although
a wellknown ancient monument, is omitted from Ordnance Survey
maps. The explanation seems to be that at the time of the first, and
early subsequent, surveys, the Kinniside Stone Circle was non-existent,
all twelve stones having long before been taken by local farmers for
use as gateposts and building materials. But forty years ago a grand
job of restoration was accomplished by an enterprising working party,
to whom great credit is due. Having cleaned out and measured the sockets
in the ground in which the stones were originally set, they searched for —
and located — the original twelve, recovered them all, and completely
restored the site. Today the circle is exactly as it was when first laid
out, thousands of years ago, waiting to surprise the next Ordnance
Survey team. *Note for survivors of the working party: one stone is loose.*

START LOCATION ....

DATE(S) WALKED ....

START TIME: .... FINISH TIME: ....

ROUTE/ASCENT(S)/DESCENT(S) USED

....

....

....

COMMENTS (walking companions, weather, observations, experiences etc)

....

....

....

....

....

from Scalehill Bridge

START LOCATION ....

DATE(S) WALKED ....

START TIME: .... FINISH TIME: ....

ROUTE/ASCENT(S)/DESCENT(S) USED

....

....

....

COMMENTS (walking companions, weather, observations, experiences etc)

....

....

....

....

....

....

....

....

....

....

....

....

START LOCATION ....

DATE(S) WALKED ....

START TIME: .... FINISH TIME: ....

ROUTE/ASCENT(S)/DESCENT(S) USED

....

....

....

COMMENTS (walking companions, weather, observations, experiences etc)

....

....

....

....

....

....

....

....

....

....

....

....

START LOCATION ....

DATE(S) WALKED ....

START TIME: .... FINISH TIME: ....

ROUTE/ASCENT(S)/DESCENT(S) USED

....

....

....

COMMENTS (walking companions, weather, observations, experiences etc)

....

....

....

....

....

....

....

CARROCK FELL

START LOCATION ....

DATE(S) WALKED ....

START TIME: .... FINISH TIME: ....

ROUTE/ASCENT(S)/DESCENT(S) USED

....

....

....

COMMENTS (walking companions, weather, observations, experiences etc)

....

....

....

....

START LOCATION ....

DATE(S) WALKED ....

START TIME: .... FINISH TIME: ....

ROUTE/ASCENT(S)/DESCENT(S) USED

....

....

....

COMMENTS (walking companions, weather, observations, experiences etc)

....

....

....

....

....

....

....

....

....

....

....

....

GOOD PLACES TO STOP, REST, EAT AND DRINK

NAME/LOCATION   COMMENTS

NAME/LOCATION   COMMENTS

GOOD PLACES TO STOP, REST, EAT AND DRINK

NAME/LOCATION   COMMENTS

NAME/LOCATION	COMMENTS

GOOD PLACES TO STOP, REST, EAT AND DRINK

NAME/LOCATION   COMMENTS

NAME/LOCATION   COMMENTS

....

....

....

....

....

....

....

....

....

....

....

....

....

....

....

....

....

....

....

....

The Lunch House

GOOD PLACES TO STOP, REST, EAT AND DRINK

NAME/LOCATION   COMMENTS

....

....

....

....

....

....

....

....

....

....

....

....

....

....

....

....

....

....

....

....

NAME/LOCATION	CHARGE	COMMENTS

GOOD PLACES TO STAY OVERNIGHT

NAME/LOCATION	CHARGE	COMMENTS

NAME/LOCATION	CHARGE	COMMENTS

Wasdale Head

GOOD PLACES TO STAY OVERNIGHT

NAME/LOCATION	CHARGE	COMMENTS

NAME/LOCATION	CHARGE	COMMENTS

Some Personal notes

Douglas fir

Douglas Fir

Scots pine

Scots Pine

Roe buck

Baby
roe deer

Sitka
spruce

Sitka Spruce

Larch

Japanese
Larch

winter

summer

PICTURE LOCATIONS AND CREDITS

The illustrations used throughout come from the following books by A. Wainwright:

Pictorial Guides to the Lakeland Fells
Book 1: The Eastern Fells
Book 2: The Far Eastern Fells
Book 3: The Central Fells
Book 4: The Southern Fells
Book 5: The Northern Fells
Book 6: The North Western Fells
Book 7: The Western Fells
The Outlying Fells of Lakeland
The Pennine Way Companion
Westmorland Heritage
A North Wales Sketchbook
A Second Lakeland Sketchbook
Scottish Mountain Drawings, The Western Highlands
Scottish Mountain Drawings, The Islands

[Publisher's Note: Where possible the location shown in the illustration is included but where no title or location was mentioned in the original book the source alone is quoted.]

Front cover: (*Book 5*)
Endpapers, front and back: (*The Pennine Way Companion*)
Title page: (*The Pennine Way Companion*)
p. 2–3 Stob Bàn 3274′, Achriabhach (*Scottish Mountain Drawings, The Western Highlands*)
p. 4 (*Book 7*)
p. 5 (*Book 5*)
p. 6 (*Book 6*)
p. 8–9 (*The Pennine Way Companion*)
p. 10 The Ravenglass and Eskdale Railway, Irton Road (*The Outlying Fells of Lakeland*)
p. 11 (*The Pennine Way Companion*)
p. 12 (*The Outlying Fells of Lakeland*)
p. 13 (*The Pennine Way Companion*)
p. 14–15 The top of Deep Gill, Scafell (*A Second Lakeland Sketchbook*)

p. 16 (*The Outlying Fells of Lakeland*)
p. 17 (*Book 4*)
p. 18–19 The mountain skyline seen from Beinn Bharrain (*Scottish Mountain Drawings, The Islands*)
p. 20 The Hanging Stone, Base Brown (*Book 7*)
p. 21 19th-century monument, Muncaster Fell (*The Outlying Fells of Lakeland*)
p. 23 Circular sheepfold, Wiley Gill, Great Calva (*Book 5*)
p. 24 Blencathra from Clough Head (*Book 1*)
p. 27 Malham Cove, Yorkshire (*The Pennine Way Companion*)
p. 29 Rock formations on Green Pikes (*The Outlying Fells of Lakeland*)
p. 30 Broad Stand, Scafell (*Book 4*)
p. 31 (*The Outlying Fells of Lakeland*)
p. 32 The Island of Rum, from the mainland (*Scottish Mountrain Drawings, The Islands*)
p. 34 Signpost, Kirkstile Inn road junction, Mellbreak (*Book 7*)
p. 36 (*The Outlying Fells of Lakeland*)
p. 37 Limestone pinnacle, Penyghent (*The Pennine Way Companion*)
p. 39 Ullswater from the north-east ridge of St. Sunday Crag (*Book 1*)
p. 40 Brae Fell from the Caldbeck road, near Fell Side (*Book 5*)
p. 42 Moss Eccles Tarn, Claife Heights (*The Outlying Fells of Lakeland*)
p. 43 Wise Een Tarn, Claife Heights (*The Outlying Fells of Lakeland*)
p. 44 The Pudding Stone, Coniston Old Man (*Book 4*)
p. 46 Swindale with Selside Pike at the head of the valley (*Book 2*)
p. 47 Swindale Head (*Book 2*)
p. 48 Path in the heather. Caldew Valley at the base of Knott (Carrock Fell in the background) (*Book 5*)
p. 51 View from Gatherstone Head, Yewbarrow (*Book 7*)
p. 52 Gray Bull, The Wet Sleddale

OTHER BOOKS BY A. WAINWRIGHT
PUBLISHED BY FRANCES LINCOLN

Walking guides (revised by Chris Jesty):
Pictorial Guides to the Lakeland Fells (available individually or as a boxed set):
    Book 1: *The Eastern Fells*; Book 2: *The Far Eastern Fells*; Book 3: *The Central Fells*;
    Book 4: *The Southern Fells*; Book 5: *The Northern Fells*; Book 6: *The North Western
    Fells*; Book 7: *The Western Fells*
The Outlying Fells of Lakeland
The Pennine Way Companion
A Coast to Coast Walk
Walks in Limestone Country
Walks on the Howgill Fells

Sketchbooks:
Lakeland Sketchbooks, Vols 1–5 (available individually or as a boxed set)
Scottish Mountain Drawings: The Western Highlands and *The Islands*
Westmorland Heritage

Other writings:
A Pennine Journey
Memoirs of a Fellwanderer
Fellwalking with Wainwright (with photographs by Derry Brabbs)
Coast to Coast with Wainwright (with photographs by Derry Brabbs)
The Wainwright Letters (edited by Hunter Davies)

Compilations:
The Best of Wainwright (selected by Hunter Davies)
Wainwright's TV Walks (introduction by Eric Robson)
Twelve Favourite Mountains
The Family Wainwright: The Southern Fells (selected by Tom Holman)
Family Walks in the Lake District: The Northern Fells (selected by Tom Holman)
The Wainwright Memorial Walk

All these books are available at www.franceslincoln.com